On The Occasion of Leroy Searle's Retirement

May 4, 2018

Printed in the United States of America.

Tautegory Press, Seattle, Washington

USA Library of Congress Control Number 2018907912

ISBN #1722227664

Table of Contents

Acknowledgments

The Departments of English and Comparative Literature hosted a retirement reception and celebration for Professor Leroy Searle on May 4, 2018, in Suzzallo Library. The event was moderated by UW English Chair Brian Reed.

This volume includes remarks made by four of Searle's colleagues as well as remarks written for the occasion by his students, colleagues and family members.

Foreword

Leroy Searle arrived at the University of Washington (UW) in the autumn of 1977. This volume focuses primarily on his teaching. His publications can be found online. Though there is no way to fully account for his service to the university and to the broader field of critical inquiry without long lists, his major accomplishments stand out.

Early in his career, Searle served three two year terms as a faculty senator (1978-1981), the last two terms as a member of the Faculty Senate Executive Committee. He was appointed associate chair of the English Department from 1982-85. He became a member of the core faculty of the Comparative History of Ideas Program in 1983.

His early interest in personal computing led him to be part of the Provost's Executive Committee on Academic Computing (1982-85), as well as chair of the IBM Project Committee in 1984-85. He founded and was first director of the Humanities and Arts Computing Center (HACC) from 1984-87. HACC morphed first into CARTAH (Center for Advanced Research in the Arts and Humanities) and since into DX-ARTS (Center for Digital Arts and Experimental Media).

Searle directed the university's College Studies Program from 1990-95. He was named the university's Arts and Sciences Liberal Arts Professor in 1994-95. He became interim director of the Center for the Humanities 1994-95, and was appointed to a five year term as director of what is now called the Simpson Center for the Humanities starting in 1995. While teaching and directing the center, Searle organized a range of conferences, including "The New Europe" (1995); "State of the Art: Criticism, Theory and the

Future of Poetry" (1997); "Fulfilling Pierce's Dream" for the International Center on Conceptual Structures (1997); "Voice, Text, and Hypertext of the Millennium" (1997); and "The Humanities Across Cultures: Theoretical Questions (1997).

He was appointed to the Provost's Task Force on Intellectual Property (1995-96), then became a member of IPMAC (the Intellectual Property Management Advisory Committee) starting in 1997-99. He served two more terms on IPMAC until he was appointed chair in 2008-2009. His committee service to the two departments of which he was a member is encyclopedic. For the Department of Comparative Literature, Searle served three terms as graduate program coordinator. He was appointed to the Joff Hanauer Honors Professorship in Western Civilization for 2008-2010.

His service extends outside the university to a range of projects. He is founding director of the Society for Critical Exchange (SCE); original managing editor of *SCE Reports* and *Critical Exchange*, published by SCE. He is a poet, photography critic, musician and composer, the founder of the Ravenna Brass Ensemble. He served as a member of the Bryant Elementary School Technology Committee in 1992, where he donated his technical services to the installation of a computer network.

Finally, Searle is the founder of Tautegory Networks, his next project which has at its foundation a large archive of material, and discourse preserved over his career, that includes an international group of participants.

Speakers

Cynthia Steele

In thinking back over my memories of Leroy over the past thirty-two years, the first cluster around the wonderful theory seminars that he and Hazard Adams organized in the late 1980s, in which they read works by particular contemporary theorists and critics together with faculty and graduate students from across the Humanities and invited those critics to campus to engage in discussions with us about their work. Invariably it was Leroy who was able to engage the visitors in greatest detail and depth; his command of literary theory was astonishing.

My second memory of Leroy is from the early 1990s, when he was directing the Center for the Humanities in its forlorn outpost in a trailer in the woods, and I taught a graduate course there about literature of Chiapas. Leroy was always coming and going with different groups of people, happily and busily overseeing the Humanities Center, which was at that time severely underfunded.

Once I transferred into the Department of Comparative Literature, my interactions with Leroy became more frequent and I had the pleasure of working closely with him as department chair and he was an indispensable Graduate Program Coordinator. His optimism and enthusiasm about student applicants to the graduate program were contagious. I remember vividly a gathering with the graduate students in the English graduate lounge, where he stepped into the kitchenette and began sautéing vegetables for the students. On another occasion an international student was going through a rough time and, after discussing the situation with me on the telephone, Leroy went over to the student's apartment late one Friday night to make sure that he was OK. Another day when I was heading into Office Depot for something, I was startled when a man on a Harley Davidson drove up to say hello; of course, it turned out to be Leroy.

From participating in a number of graduate exams and dissertation defenses with him, I learned that, if you expect the best of the students, you will rarely be disappointed. When Leroy disagreed with me on some policy point regarding the students or the department, he was never shy about sitting down with me and discussing the matter at length. Once when we locked horns, he stopped me in my tracks by saying, "There are two prickly people in this room, and I'm one of them." Many of our conversations were enlivened by other of Leroy's homey philosophical sayings, reminding me of his roots in Midwestern farming country, which it was easy to forget when he was holding forth of any of countless philosophical topics.

At department meetings over the years, no matter what has transpired during the meeting, we have rarely parted without a reminder from Leroy about how fortunate we are to be in such a congenial department.

I'm grateful to him for his undaunted optimism, for his unshakable belief in students, for his wide-ranging and formidable intellect. I have no doubt that, in retirement, Leroy will keep sending out roots in new directions and delighting us in a thousand unpredictable ways.

Gary Handwerk

I had thought, on composing these remarks, to show more deference to Leroy's own characteristic style. But I've always had my own preference, especially on occasions like this one, for comments that are short and organized. So, four points.

1) Leroy as Scholar and Intellectual: I have, over the course of my academic career, had the privilege of knowing perhaps six people who were genuine polymaths, people who seem somehow to know something about everything, people whose breadth of knowledge is matched by an equivalent depth. Leroy is one of those people, with an active, curious intellect I have never ceased to admire. As one instance among many I could cite, Leroy's headnotes to the edition of literary theory texts that he co-edited with Hazard Adams are remarkable, drawing on a wealth of knowledge to which I can only aspire. The logical conclusion from this: it would, I think, be foolhardy to engage Leroy in a game of trivia on any subject at all. Even given the chance to choose a topic I'd deem safe, such as the early history of the Baltimore Orioles baseball franchise (since I don't know Leroy to be much of a baseball fan), I feel certain that he would somehow, from depths of unanticipated wisdom, turn out to know far more than I did about this. So, a caution. Never play trivia with Leroy.

2) Leroy as Teacher and Mentor: As a teacher, Leroy is—as students and colleagues all know—flat-out insane. To look at any syllabus from a class he teaches is to have as inevitable reaction: "O my gawd! How could anybody even *imagine* teaching that in a single quarter?" But somehow, it worked, time after time, year after year. Leroy did imagine like this, and student after student across multiple generations rose to the challenges he set…and remember him to this day as one of the most influential teachers they have ever had.

3) Leroy as Colleague and Departmental Citizen: Having

had the rare opportunity to be Leroy's department chair not once, but twice—in both Comparative Literature and English—I grew familiar with a side of Leroy about which his colleagues doubtless know less than they should. Leroy has across his entire career been an extraordinarily generous and dedicated departmental member, never just doing his prescribed tasks, but always the first to offer to take on an extra class, to devise a new syllabus, to work on a challenging dissertation committee—anything whatsoever. He was, moreover, selfless in this, asking no recompense, expecting no reward, just doing things like this because they were the right things to do.

4) Anecdote: And finally, the obligatory anecdote. I recall going up to Leroy after a contentious department meeting in English that I had chaired (though the adjective may be redundant in this context), and having Leroy look me in the eye and say, "That was the worst-chaired department meeting I have ever been in." I think he was wrong; I'm confident I chaired meetings more badly than that particular one. But I report this not just as a measure of Leroy's characteristic bluntness and sincerity. I report it because in that aftermath of this encounter, Leroy never displayed any residual animosity, nor did he alter his behavior toward me in any way. That meeting was over; it was done, and there were no grudges to be held, no vengeance to be enacted. For all his passion (and there was often a great deal of it), Leroy showed a remarkable tolerance for his opponents, in ways that I'm not sure all of them fully realized.

It has been a privilege and a pleasure to work—for some thirty years now—alongside Leroy in all his many roles. I hope and trust that he won't leave us completely, that we will continue to see him on campus and in Padelford Hall. And I wish him the best of all lives in his retirement.

Bob Abrams

Begin: quote from Ralph Ellison's *Invisible Man*. The marvelously multifaceted Rinehart:

"Could he be all if them? Rine the runner and Rine the gambler and Rine the briber and Rine the lover and Rinehart the Reverend? . . . He was broad man, a man of parts who got around. Rinehart the rounder. It was true as I was true. His world was possibility and he knew it."

Leroy—his world is possibility, and he knows it

Leroy the Motorcyclist

Leroy the Mechanic

Leroy the Musician

Leroy the Chef

Leroy the multifaceted scholar and teacher: From the Qur'an to Hawthorne, from British Romanticism to Charles Sanders Peirce, and on and on and on………

Met Hazard Adams one day in the mail room. I mentioned to Hazard: hey, I just discovered that Leroy plays trumpet……… Hazard back to me: that's just a small, small part of it. And then Hazard begins to list numerous abilities, interests, capacities, all of which define Leroy Searle.   And then—after a moment of silence--Hazard flashes me an oracular look, turns around, and walks off……………… and from way down the hall I hear: "You've just been acquainted with infinity."

COWS. Background…. We're a national and, increasingly, an international, global department……………….. On the face of it, we all walk the walk and talk the talk of Academe, and it's easy to forget that we come from massively different backgrounds. But one afternoon, don't know how it started, but up on the 4th floor hallway of Padelford, Leroy, from Utah, shocked me out of my parochial New York upbringing by informing me that I didn't know a damned thing about cows.

My New York version of a cow is Elsie the cow in the old Borden's Dairy advertisements. She's sweet. She has lovely eyelashes. Her world is fresh air and daisies. You'd see her picture in subway stations, on milk cartons in neighborhood grocery stores, on TV—she was a New York favorite, and Elsie pretty much summed up for me the delight and beauty of cows.

Well, in any event, Leroy—and then Brian, who stepped out his fourth-floor office and joined the conversation—proceeded to disabuse me with all the authority of two country boys from Utah and Kentucky who know cows only too well. Cows kick you, I'm told. They're ornery. They're grumpy. They smell. They can be stubborn. What did I know about cows?

I was cowed. ……………….. And it dawned on me that after a trip with my PS 22, second-grade class to a cheese factory in Long Island City just over the bridge from Manhattan, I actually thought that cheese was made in factories……………….

Now, Leroy the motorcyclist!

Back in the day, we served on numerous committees ---the Undergraduate Education Committee, the Graduate Studies Committee, this committee, that committee—and sometimes committee meetings lasted until 5 PM.   Leroy always had a lot to say, and I was inevitably impressed with his grasp of budgets, of politics down in Olympia, of why faculty shoot themselves in the foot in their ignorance of these matters.

But my Leroy fantasy (I really, really hope it's true) goes like this. The committee meeting breaks. We all go down to the Padelford Hall garage, get into our Hondas and Subaru station wagons and head home—all, that is, except Leroy. Unlike the rest of us, Leroy gets on his motorcycle, revs it up, roars north on 25 Avenue...................... and in the middle of afternoon traffic, does the most glorious wheelie that you could ever imagine.................

Well, Leroy.   Perhaps your wheelies are now more metaphoric than literal........... Indeed, all of us, when we reach a certain age, learn to transition from the literal to the metaphoric, and we seek to cultivate this art as best we can. ....

If now only metaphor, I wish you the most glorious of wheelies—a long, long string of them, for a long time to come..............

I salute you, my friend.   I say this with all my heart: it has been my pleasure—and my great honor—to have been your colleague for all these years.

Sam Hushagen

I will try to keep my comments short, since I can really only underscore what has already been said about Leroy.

Last summer, I was about two miles from home when my motorcycle broke down, leaving me stranded on the side of the road. As I was walking back to my house, I called a handful of mechanics, none of whom wanted to risk working on an 30 year old bike. Not sure what to do, or how I was going to get my bike from off the side of the busy road where I'd left it, I called Leroy. He told me he would be at my house with his motorcycle trailer in about an hour.

As I watched Leroy pull up in his pickup I wondered how many doctoral candidates could call their dissertation chair and ask for roadside assistance. Long conversations about employment prospects, wrangling over difficult conceptual issues, sure. But mechanical assistance?

I bring this up because it is emblematic of the care and generosity that define Leroy's mentorship. It goes so far beyond the kind of academic support and guidance that most graduate students are looking for when we seek out a chair. As all of Leroy's students here can attest, his investment in our health and well-being of us is exemplary. His care isn't restricted to office hour visits or marginal comments on chapter drafts. In fact, I don't think I've ever had an "office hour" meeting with Leroy that ran fewer than three hours. It is hard to imagine in his 30 years at the University of Washington how many slices of apple and halves of bagels Leroy has pushed across that table in the HUB in the direction of stressed, famished students.

I first met Leroy ten years ago, in spring term of 2008. I was writing my undergraduate thesis, on William Carlos Williams's "Spring and All." I was struggling, and my official adviser recommended I talk to someone with a better command of the text. She gave me Leroy's name and I shot him an email that tried to lay out my project and the theoretical thickets I was stuck in. I had never taken a class with Leroy. I'd never even met him. He sent me a response two hours later, asking if I was available to meet him in the HUB the next day. When I arrived I sat down and started to talk a mile a minute and Leroy let me keep going until, sliding half an apple across the table he told me to slow down, and asked me, "How much do you know about Immanuel Kant?" We met weekly that quarter, talking for hours each time. And since that first meeting I couldn't count the hours he has invested in my undergraduate and graduate education giving feedback, direction, and advice, to say nothing of the home-cooked meals.

I often quote one of my favorite of Leroy's adages. Most of you have probably heard it before. "Whenever someone asks you what you teach, tell them 'students'". It's a bit smartass, but when Leroy says it, it isn't a quick retort. Rather, it's a challenge to know and value and respect the students that take your classes, whose papers you read and whose comments and questions that as a teacher you work to educe. In the ten years I have known Leroy, through innumerable conversations, always punctuated by the move from the Atrium to the upper tables at 5, through dinners and holiday parties at the Searle residence, and even a cross-country red eye, I have learned as much about compassion and humanity in teaching as I have about Plato, Kant, and Coleridge.

To close, I would like to take a card from the deck of another recently retired mentor, Marshall Brown. As you all know, Marshall is fond of quoting from whomever he is introducing or toasting.

In a 2006 essay in MLN, Leroy writes: "The pursuit of professionalism, the interminable publication of essays that no one reads, of books needed to get tenure which no one, not even the libraries, buy is, in Guillory's account, a kind of a pyramid scheme of publication for its own sake, for survival in a profession that has been under assault not only from elected officials who must vote for the budgets (and really do not know what we do and why it should matter) but from ourselves, unable to get our own departments in order, as we keep on accepting more graduate students and producing PhDs (at the risk of sounding cynical) at least as much to maintain a pool of cheap labor for the moment (and a captive audience for our advanced research) as to provide well trained teachers for the future." Now, I quote this grim assessment of the profession because as anyone who has had a long conversation with Leroy knows, forms of scholarly communication and prospects for employment are bound to come up. Leroy has often said in conversation that one of the benefits of longevity is perspective.

But what is peculiar about Leroy's perspective is that it is not grim by any measure. In such institutionally inauspicious times, when the status of English departments and humanities study more generally has never seemed more imperiled, or more precarious, Leroy sees possibilities there, just at the horizon of visibility. Leroy's restless curiosity and enthusiasm, his imaginative vitality even after 30 years of this work, his erudition and depth, his uncanny sense of knowing exactly what you should be reading before you do, are an endless source of inspiration. I have had conversations with other grad students in the winding halls of Padelford about the peculiar effect of conversations with Leroy: in spite of precariousness, in spite of uncertainty and insecurity, we come out of those conversations with a renewed sense of vocation, with an excitement about our projects, and with an indelible sense that our work is valued.

And so, in closing, I would like to say thank you, Leroy, for all those boiled eggs and apple slices, for "deeply human and humane care," to quote you once again, that you have shown your undergraduate and graduate students. I wish you and Annie a happy, restful, and productive retirement. And I hope you'll send me an advance copy of *Plato, Aristotle and the Poets*. Congratulations.

Contributors

Eric Ames

What a privilege it has been to work with you these past few years. Thank you for making me feel so at home in CLCM!

Jonathan Arac

On the occasion of celebrating your retirement, I remember my remarkable good fortune in beginning to know you at Princeton back in the mid 1970s, through the good will of Earl Miner. The Society for Critical Exchange was an important counterpoint to *boundary 2* in my own course of learning to think about a whole range of things we care about, and you proved the most compelling mind of those I encountered through SCE. I still have vivid memories of my visit to UW and the hospitality you and Annie extended back in 1981. So many years passed and so many fewer times together than I would have wished for, but it was a great gift to have the time with James that I did while he was at CMU.

The world is richer for your being here, and I'll be very glad to see you whenever the next chance happens.

Jacinthe Assad

From conversation to conversation, across coffee shops from the U-District and UW, to Capitol Hill and Queen Anne, your words have not only shaped my journey as a scholar, but I realize in retrospect that they also trace significant milestones in my personal journey, from the good and the bad, to the exhilarating and the life-changing. You have stood by me through it all!

Now, an ocean across, a continent apart, and what seems like a lifetime away, your words resonate all the more. And I long for them.

You pass on strength and compassion, wisdom and guidance, without which I don't know how to evaluate my experience in the US, and beyond. I have cried and laughed with you, shared a constellation of aspirations and dreams, and you have supported me along every step. And I know, from talking to others, that I am not alone in expressing this reality.

Your dedication, understanding, commitment, and compassion to your students truly are remarkable and have touched all those who crossed your path.

I am grateful that you have opened up your mind and heart to me, to us. You and Annie share your home and your succulent meals like we're family. That generosity is more than eloquent.

And I'm not even speaking on a professional level! Had I remained in academia, I would have strived to be half the professor you are. I pity the generations of students who will not take a class with Leroy, on poetry, on theory, on literature, on music… I believe that they will miss it without quite knowing what it is they're missing.

Your readiness and thirst for knowledge are an inspiration. You take on new intellectual and challenging projects with an ease I envy.

I am not sure how academia will survive without you! I do, however, know how you can survive without it. Music, cooking, motorbikes, and so much more. I have no worries that your days will be happily filled with even more wonders.

And wonders they are! I do hope that I will see you again, so we can talk and talk and talk. And listen to music and eat!

Happy retirement, dear Leroy. You deserve it! Know that you have unleashed onto the world an army of critical cultural agents and intellectuals, who will do no less than change their part of the world. Because of you.

With so much love and admiration.

Tani Barlow

I worked with Leroy for 14 years. I arrived at UW with a journal, the promise of a room for the journal and a computer to run the journal plus an RA to help out. When I arrived the office turned out to be a corner cubicle of the old Temporary Quonset hut, the nice computer that the secretary had had until it got snatched from her and given to me. In other words I had not understood that I should have agreed to "an office with a door and a new computer" before I signed the contract. Leroy took me under his wing. He taught me a lesson that I never forgot. Tani, he said, "always think like a rat." In other words how to get the cheese requires a quick mind, a stable objective and stealth combined with big teeth. I know that Leroy will never stop thinking like a rat and neither will I. Congratulations, Leroy Searle!!!

Yomi Braester

I'll miss our many discussions. Thanks for your generosity through the years (and don't ride that motorcycle!)

Mikkel Borch-Jacobsen

Run comrade, the old world is behind you!

Marshall Brown

May you be as happy in retirement as you have made so many students and colleagues for decades.

Lin Chen

Studying in the US was once a college dream I held dear to my heart. Restless and cynical, I was looking for a different educational experience than the one I had in China, the best of its kind in the world: famous professors, beautiful campus, fellow students equally passionate about what they study, endless academic books that represent the pinnacle of wisdom humans can attain. That dream has largely come true. I did get to know a few superstar academics, love the campuses I studied at, get along with others in the academy, and come across a few books that have made me wiser than before. But midway through that educational journey, something important already felt missing, something more important to a student than perhaps everything else combined, but which I still find hard to put into words: probably a desire for belief in the goodness of human nature, a feeling of intimacy necessary to the flourishing of a teacher-student relationship, a wish that knowledge would not only lead to worldly success, but also a morally good life. It was you, Leroy, who made me feel full again. To me, you are not only a kind teacher, but a fatherly figure, a source of joy and courage and hope. Without you I might not have endured to the end and be "saved." Please take very good care of your precious self after retirement, and do keep in touch.

Sima Daad

Please accept my warm congratulations on your great accomplishment of academic service you have provided to several generations of students including myself. Being an international student from a country that has had many complications with the US government at the expense of its citizens' life, I went through a myriad of challenges at social, existential, intellectual, academic and cultural levels. But you were always there with your wisdom and insightful guidance. Now, looking back to those years and hardships I should admit that if it was not for your help, I would have hardly been able to make it happen. You have indeed set a role model for me and many others for humane professionalism and integrity. UW community must be missing you. Thank you, thank you, thank you.

Colleen Donnelly

We meet few people in our lives who truly impact who we become. Leroy is one of those people for me, more than a professional mentor, he taught those privileged to work with him how to expand the ways they think. He challenged us not to be confined by single fields and philosophies so that we fit academic paradigms and expectations but rather encouraged us to break boundaries, to see consonances, to develop our intellectual acuity. Those of us who often felt like outsiders for thinking differently or challenging normative ideologies, he inspired and guided, as we explored the novelty of our ideas, while grounding us in well-established traditions and theories. He encouraged our enthusiasm, softened our setbacks, and heartily praised and helped us celebrate our accomplishments; we reveled in his warmth and humanity. We embody what he gifted us and can only hope to pass his legacy on, as his disciples, to future generations.

Amal Eqeiq

To Leroy: Santa Comes Everyday

It was on a typical nebulous day in early September of 2006 when Yuko told me: "He will be waiting for you at the coffee shop in the Hub. He looks like Santa!" I was still new to Seattle and still getting used to many new cultural shocks: being so far up north way from Palestine, not using an umbrella when it rains, and looking for Santa in September. When I left Seattle in 2013, these new realities became metaphysical conditions: the remoteness of life at the edge of the map, walking wet in the rain, and seeing Santa all year round and in different positions: on a vagabond motor- bike, in a literature seminar, in the kitchen roasting a thick steak for a big party, and across the coffee table in the Hub listening patiently as I orally narrate all of my 9 incomplete final seminar papers that I have not written due to a combination of chronic procrastination, a resentment of highbrow academic prose, and an anguish about not writing in my voice. On October 2012, Santa delivered an early Christmas gift. He helped me get to a job interview with Williams College. "You need to go, even if it is only for a one-year visiting assistant professor position. Williams is a great school and you make a good impression in person," he said enthusiastically. Six years have passed since then and I am now finishing my second-year as a tenure-track Assistant Professor of Arabic Studies and Comparative Literature at Williams College. When people ask me how I got here, I tell them: "With a little help from Santa!" Thank you, Leroy! Thank you for all the lessons that you have taught us about the relevance of literature in shaping an ethical imagination in all times, and especially during times of crisis. And thank you for being part of a radical vision that recognizes the persistent need to study the humanities because it is the fertile field where we cultivate hope.

Cassandra Searle Ewer (Daughter)

I can't remember a time when my dad was not teaching. Whether it was teaching at the University, or with us at home, or while we were driving in the car, or even as we were fishing on a lake in the middle of a forest in a boat that we "borrowed" since the boat rental attendant seemed to be nowhere in attendance (Leroy was always doing slightly disreputable things, but he did it with such authority that it didn't even occur to us to question it), he was continually instructing us and encouraging us to learn.

Often these teaching moments came in the form of stories, some of which were slightly horrifying tales from his youth which delighted us and made us giggle at the time, but which I wasn't sure I would share with my own children. At the age of 12, my son Matthew spent a summer with Leroy building computers. I asked Matthew what he remembered about his time with grandpa. "I remember him telling me inappropriate jokes" Matthew said, laughing uproariously. He remembered a great many other experiences, most of them centered around the fascination of learning how to do something really cool.

Of course I did share all those stories with my kids (I figured they were great cautionary tales regardless), and we still laugh about his stories and the practical jokes he played in his youth...my boys were fascinated by the idea of setting fire to a sack of cow manure on someone's porch, ringing the doorbell and hiding. They wanted to try it immediately. In my own youth, I heard these stories so often that my sister

Sabrina and I joked that we should just number them and save time - "number 34! Hahahaha!"

Sabrina and I soon realized that Leroy's love of teaching through stories extended to sharing stories about our own childhood with his graduate students. My sister and I became minor celebrities, particularly at department events and gatherings for his students. I was a born performer who craved the spotlight so I loved the fame...until about the age of 13, when I decided I would rather that he not tell his students about the embarrassingly stupid things I did as a child, no matter how charming they seemed. I confess that now, as a teacher myself, I use my own children's stories shamelessly.

All the stories, projects in the workshop, road trips to visit historic landmarks, conversations late at night, and the hundreds of other Leroy experiences I had throughout my life have had a common theme...it is simply kick-butt FUN to know things. I love to learn! And I know that this intense desire for knowledge, the joy of learning new things and teaching others was fostered fundamentally by my dad.

It tickles me to think of the hundreds (probably thousands) of students he has taught over the years. And I know that his retirement from university teaching will not stop him from continuing to teach and learn; it is intrinsically part of his DNA. I can't wait to see what new projects he has in store!

Best of luck, Leroy. I love you and am immensely proud of you.

Paul Jaussen

Since I won't be able to make Leroy's retirement, I wanted

to send along a few words. I've kept them brief, as I'm sure there will be many who have things to say!

Leroy is a champion of intellectual and imaginative freedom. As a reader, writer, and teacher, he is equal parts generative and generous, provocative and collaborative, encouraging and enlivening. Working alongside him, both as a graduate student and teaching assistant, was one of the great privileges of my life, and I know that there are generations of students who feel the same way.

Sevim Kebeli & Murat Inan

Currently in Ankara, Turkey

We first met Leroy Searle in our Comparative Literature class in 2008. Since then Prof. Searle has broadened our understanding of literary theory and has encouraged us to relate our research to a broader network of world literature. He has always emphasized the fact that without comparing we cannot truly understand what something really is.

The amazing support he has shown to his students has been very special. He has nourished his students not only intellectually but also with great food, coffee and conversation.

He always supported our academic journey through the ups and downs we experienced: he always made time for us and supported our work.

Leroy is a great scholar and an outstanding theoretical thinker. But more importantly, he is a compassionate, genuine, and kind human being.

Thank you, Leroy, for everything and our best wishes to you

as you start a new chapter of your life.

Alvin Kwiram

I am disappointed that I will miss this event because I will be out of town at an Advisory Board meeting. I wish to convey my warmest best wishes to Leroy for this next phase of his life. It was always a pleasure working with him.

Anita Searle Manning (Sister)

I don't think I will be able to make it to Leroy's retirement celebration. I do, however, have a couple of things to say.

I am the youngest in the family. Our parents expected me to be a boy. In fact, they were so certain that they hadn't thought of any girls names. So when Leroy's little brother George turned out to be a girl, they were completely at a loss. Only Leroy and our sister Evelyn were old enough to visit mom in the hospital. There were rules about such things back then. She loved to tell me how excited they were when they came in and told her Leroy had a name for the baby. Anita. Mom remembered it as being someone from a book he was reading at the time. Whether that was the case or not isn't really important because it was so fitting for him.

He was an example to me from the very beginning. When I was about 8 or 9 and told him I wanted to write a book when I grew up, he didn't laugh or tell me that was silly. He was very thoughtful and encouraging. He told me when I was ready he would help me. That will not be a surprise to anyone who knows him.

Congratulations to the best big brother ever. I can't wait to see what the next chapter holds for you.

Katy Masuga

How did I get so lucky? How did I even find you, I wonder, or you me, Leroy Searle? Look at all of us around you whose eyes glisten with gratitude, love and wonder. You are exceptional, and that is something we have the honor of carrying with us our entire lives. You raise the bar, Leroy, and you help us to meet it and raise it also. You have shown me what is possible--not just in research, career, perseverance, ambition but in compassion, equanimity, patience, spirit. I have so, so much in my heart for you. And I know what you've done there, sir. I know what you've done, what you're doing for us: giving so we can give; an endless, vital, priceless giving that teaches us how to give, in turn, to others and even to ourselves. The university owes not an insignificant number of cultivated minds to you, and I am personally indebted for so much more, down to the shoes on my feet --not to mention: a repaired head gasket, distributor cap, and trumpet valves, to say nothing of the elaborate meals, gatherings, meetings, conversations and coffees, a roof over my head as needed, cold medicine, mail collection, rides to the airport, babysitting if needed, and anywhere-anytime life and grief counseling. So much more could be added! I hope this retirement opens a new chapter for you of well deserved rest and self-care and focus. Thank you, Leroy. I love you dearly.

Yuko Mera

Thank you for all your support throughout the years. Wishing you all the best in your next chapter. I know you'll be busy with all your projects. Congratulations!

Kathy Mork

I've only been able to claim having known and worked with you for 35 of the past years. Remember HAL, the computer you built in the mid-80's? Thank goodness many of us figured out how to turn on our computers. That's nothing compared to the many great, deep conversations we've had. Looking forward to many more!

Yasi Naraghi

Thank you for all of your support throughout the years. Happy retirement!

Sean O'Connor

I must admit I have a narrow perspective on the amazing contributions that Leroy Searle has made to the UW, but one that is worth highlighting. Outside of his tenured subject matter expertise, Leroy was an insightful repository of invaluable institutional knowledge about faculty and staff IP policies. He was a longstanding member of IPMAC (the IP Management Advisory Committee) and I worked with him first as a fellow committee member and then as Chair. I quickly came to trust and defer to the deep knowledge Leroy had about our IP policy, history, and values. He also was always willing to consider other perspectives and would listen, before offering thoughtful commentary. We came close to creating a new and beneficial IP policy to replace the current antiquated one, but, due in large part to my taking an overdue sabbatical, that was not to be—at least for now. Someone should make sure they sit down with Leroy and capture his wisdom and insights before he goes off to a well-deserved retirement. Or perhaps, with luck, we will be able to reach out to him in this next phase of his life for insights as we hopefully move towards a more equitable and just IP policy for ALL of our stakeholders at UW.

I will miss him and wish I could have been there today.

Melek Ortabasi

I'm sorry I can't be there to help you celebrate your retirement. You, retired, is hard to picture: I always imagine you with that characteristic smile on your face, thinking out loud about some new and interesting concept or idea; never bored, never idle. It is this quality of yours that made you such a welcome addition to my dissertation committee. As someone working on two wildly divergent literary traditions, German and Japanese, it was often difficult to feel like I "fit in" somewhere. But you always made me feel like I was onto something, like I had something new to say, something important to contribute to the field. And guess what: you were right. Thanks to you, my belief in positive thinking survived those existential grad school years. I'm forever grateful for your unstinting support and belief in my ability. It has made a big difference.

Here's to many more adventures to come. But hopefully not involving motorcycles.

Sabrina Searle Porter (Daughter)

I'm sure many of Leroy's students can relate to the feeling that his expectations are high and the homework is daunting. In 1973, my sister and I (ages 9 and 6) were required to watch the hearings of Watergate instead of reruns of our favorite show, "The Flying Nun." We were to bring newspaper articles to dinner for discussion, read instead of watch TV (always), and defend our comments and ideas with full-fledged logic. So, if you have been a student of Leroy's, I feel your pain! But I'm sure we would all agree that we are better for having had the opportunity to catch a glimpse of the way Leroy thinks things ought to be done.

Leroy is a teacher from head to toe. His drive to teach has little to do with his advanced degrees and decades in a University setting. He is a teacher because he has utter confidence in what he knows and has the generosity of spirit to want to share it.   As I think back over my life and the many things he taught me, the list is impressive indeed. From an early age the most important lesson was to "pay attention" – to pretty much everything that was going on around me and in the world in general. I think I did learn to pay attention and that skill has served me well in a wide variety of situations over the past 5 decades. As I grew, the instruction became more specific and included important skills like cutting meat with a "real" knife - since all 5-year olds ought to handle knives competently. Leroy taught me how to ride a bike, take a photo and develop it in a darkroom, shoot a basketball, explore a junk store (and befriend the owner), refinish furniture, type on a manual typewriter, understand the way computer language works, use a variety of power tools including, but not limited to; belt sander, soldering iron, blow torch, printing press, and a table saw. As a teenager, when I was feeling down, Leroy would offer to take me to the dump to "slug rats". I never did take him up on that offer, but it was a testament to the endless skills of Leroy and his sensitivity to offer them up at just the right moment!

Each learning opportunity seemed to be part of a very serious undertaking with the net effect of showing me that there really wasn't anything I couldn't figure out if I worked at it. The teaching happened because Leroy was engaged in something and took the opportunity and the time to include me in the adventure. In so doing, he communicated to me that, of course, I could do anything and that all of what we don't yet understand is just out there waiting to be tackled. Leroy has the unique ability to bring people along for the ride. His own interests and enthusiasm to understand new things are powerful and energizing for everyone, his children included.

In retrospect, I recall that fishing was just about the only "past time" we did with Dad where his intensity dropped to a low hum as we patiently and methodically drowned many, many worms every summer. Dad told us jokes while we fished and for the most part we managed to "keep tension on the line" while simultaneously working on our summer tans.

At 52 years old, I don't have many friends whose fathers have just retired. I'm not surprised at all that Leroy chose to continue his time at the University more than 10 years past the "normal" retirement age. In fact, I find that not much has changed in the way I think of Leroy as I imagine his life going forward. If you know Leroy, you know that his interests are so expansive that this next phase will surely be another chapter in a life chock-full of discovery.

I love you Dad.

Mary Searle Rockwood (Sister)

As another of Leroy's sisters I would like to add my two cents.

Having an older brother like Leroy has been a pleasure all my life. As a kid he seemed to me so tall and strong, someone worthy of admiration. I did indeed admire him. As

I grew older I found even more to admire. He has always been an example of strength and integrity. His curiosity and boundless energy are awe inspiring.

Leroy always seemed to do so many different thing in addition to his job I have no doubt he will keep every bit as busy in retirement as he has always been.

Good on ya, bro!

Sarah Ross

Every chat has been a pleasure – I hope many more will come. Thank you for insisting on William Carlos Williams -- reading his work ten years later was indeed a joy. I wish you many fulfilling days to come – time for new projects!

David Shields

Leroy, I've long admired your independence, integrity, rigor, and polymathic brilliance.

Zach Tavlin

Your Blake class was the first I took at UW. You crashed your bike, had surgery and came in the next day. And ready to teach the Zoas no less. A wonderful chair, come visit in Chicago sometime.

Jenny Van Houdt

I write to (of course) thank you for all your support over the years. While I cannot express it more eloquently than Sam, your generosity as a mentor is unmatched in this program. More than the food and coffee (which I am also grateful for), I have not received so much *time* from a single individual in my entire college experience. The hours alone not only speak to your dedication to your students and their ideas, but your dogged pursuit of smart, rigorously interrogated ideas. No one has challenged me more, nor asked harder, more foundational questions. Your main question in my exams became the best chapter of my dissertation (in my opinion, at least). I look forward to dissecting the central problem you raised in my defense and mulling it over *for the next few years.* Thank you for all your support and forgive me the awful dog pun!

Rob Weller

Well Leroy, I never really believed this day would arrive. I can't thank you enough for your support and enthusiasm. My life would be far different and probably in Walla Walla if not for you.

Susan Williams

I remember how hard you worked to convince us that yes, we did need to learn to use computers. Wish I'd paid more attention!

Shawn Wong

I think we should've gotten you a Harley accessory instead of this book as you ride off into the sunset. Well, as our recent literature Nobel Laureate once said, "Don't look back."

Response

Leroy F. Searle

May 4, 2018

Thank you all for coming. It is, today, 41 years since I returned a signed contract with the University of Washington, almost no details of which I can remember. What was clear, however, was that having served a 7 year sentence at a select private liberal arts university, saturated in money, and thinking altogether too well of itself, it was a relief to be, in a manner of speaking, back in the mainstream of American higher education, part of perhaps the most ambitious and worthwhile experiment ever, to try to educate all the children of all the people. For that, I am immeasurably grateful, to my colleagues, so many of whom are elsewhere; to the university, never awash in money but which has proved itself time and again to be a place of real possibilities; but most of all to my students, thousands of them, but especially in the last decade, graduate students who are, without exaggeration, the best I have ever taught: Zach, Sam, Yasi, Brad, Patrick, Rene, Jacob, Nathaniel, Devin—there are more—all facing the accumulated effects of administrative and institutional clumsiness that appears to have no clear way to confront the fact that the financial model that has so far kept the doors open has been largely dysfunctional for arguably longer than the same decade. We all know that this is no merely local problem, and that what it will take to sort out is all but unimaginable. But there is the point: we are not going to engineer or calculate our way out of it, and no shifty transfer of tuition dollars to the construction of buildings that aside from rentable residential real estate, will have more effect on parking than on the everyday, essential work for which we all signed up: As Chaucer put it, in praise of his humble Clerk of Oxenford-- 'gladly would he learn and gladly teach'. How are we to do that now? Of course this is an ancient issue, not in itself ever meant to be profitable, but having as its only purpose to allow us, induce us, sometimes force us, to think, to reflect, to pay attention to the marvels of what is right before us. We have to imagine it, and if we think that means to indulge in fantasy or celebrate the rectitude of our politics, we will have missed the point.

What I take to be so important in the students here, right now, is precisely that with all they have to concern them, they *have* looked at what is right before them: these texts, these poems and stories, musical compositions and works of art, conceptual tangles, that familiar though they be, are inexhaustible, urgent, and still unknown. It cannot be news to anyone in this room that our mode of organizing our affairs—colleges, divisions, all with their respective Deans; departments, all with their curricula, staff, mud wrestling with budgets, hiring freezes, absolutely bizarre practices by which we encounter the seven arcana of scheduling a room and assigning a teacher so that the students who keep coming, wave upon wave, will at least have a place to sit—that all of this has to change. But our graduate students, right now, *right now*, faced with that kind of uncertainty, have nevertheless managed to see what is interesting, what is not yet clearly thought, in old books and new, that continues to confront us, not with answers but with a more urgent injunction: *what about this? What do you make of this peculiar thing?* And then to pursue it, though at the very door is some frightful gong poised to deliver the crack of doom, they read, they write, they revise, so as to see, so as to experience not meaning as some property of things that will just be given to us, but as an event, a happening, that does open doors, lets in light.

In going through the long list of things that have to be done to get out of here, longer it seems than the list of things that had to be done to get in, I have kept thinking about two things, two recollections, one the earliest clear, narrative memory I have, the other a bit of text from a book of poems by a friend from graduate school, with an odd sense that they are connected. In 1945, shortly after I had turned 3, Walt Disney re-issued his massive film, *Pinocchio*, which I have ever since regarded as one of the most horrifying films ever made; I will shortly tell you why. Until about 8 years ago, I had not read Carlo Collodi's original tale—and I did so, while teaching a graduate seminar in modern poetry where, to my surprise, I had virtually the entire population of graduate students form Romance Languages—the reason? There appeared to be no other seminars available where French or Italian poems were on the slate. I realized when pointed to the original by one of the students that this classic of Disnification *was* a dark, dark tale. But at 3, just after the war was over, my mother was so pleased to be able to take the kids to this gala re-issue, so as I sat there, in the stately Capitol Theater in Salt Lake City, what met me was the repetition of a pattern that upset me more than anything I can think of since: in every episode, Pinocchio would lie, his nose would grow longer, and he would get farther and farther away from home. I recall it like an internal shout: NO, NO Pinocchio, don't do it: with every lie, your nose will grow longer and you will be even more hopelessly lost. Finally I took my mother's hand and dragged her, as well as a 3 year old could, out to the lobby, insisting that we just go home. I recall her, as I sat on the lobby bench, on her tip toes to look in the window of the swinging door, wanting to see the movie—and she took me back in, to see Pinocchio tell another lie.

I still have the same reaction, embarrassingly enough, often in department meetings, administrative sessions: Don't do it, don't do it. But now it is that, what we are here to do is the modest thing, to read, to write, to think, in the relative safety of a place ostensibly dedicated to exactly that. When we don't do it, things go badly.

But the second thought has been of an epigraph to Jim Dodge's privately printed first book *de Vaca in a Vanishing Geography*. When I first read it, I was stunned. Cabeza de Vaca, having led a tiny band of lost Spaniards from the Gulf of Mexico on an 8 year journey across the entire country, and safely back to the Spanish encampment. Here's the epigraph:

". . . the power of maintaining life in others lives within each of us, and from each of us does it recede when unused. It is a concentrated power. If you are not acquainted with it, your Majesty can have no inkling of what it is like, what it portends, or the ways in which it slips from one."

That is it: it is what we have to do, and what our students have immediately before them. And it is worth everything.

Afterword

James H.S. Searle

I spent the morning listening to the recordings of Leroy Searle's retirement ceremony yesterday, which I missed because the semester is still going full steam out East. Thanks to all who attended, spoke, or sent in remarks; it was immensely moving to hear. There is too much to say about Leroy as a teacher, a thinker, a father, and as a person; I will spare him the embarrassment (at least for now) of writing anything too long or detailed. I have been so fortunate to have parents who avoided paternalism, led by example more than by force, and who always treated me as a full and complex person free to make mistakes and find my way. The longer I live, the more aware I am of my privilege and luck to have grown up with both Annie and Leroy. They opened their home to students and colleagues, filled it with books, conversation, music, and ideas and encouraged me to speak up and participate.

Growing up in Seattle it was relatively common for me to meet a stranger who had a story about Leroy saving them in a pinch—from automotive repair to a family crisis—as well as an argument for why my father was a wizard or genius. The remarkable thing is that somehow each of these anecdotes revealed another strata or facet of my father. It is such a joyous thing to come to know more of your loved ones through the reports of thankful and enthusiastic strangers.

Hazard's quip about Leroy embodying infinity is spot on. When you get close to my father, you recognize that his seemingly boundless energy does not emanate from some private source but is a consequence of his involvement with the world and the persons, ideas, and traditions it produces continuously. He has shown me how necessary it is to be concerned with long, big, and complicated problems. He has also taught many of us the value of power tools and pocket knives, improvisational cooking, the importance of making things with your hands, and of taking more time than seems possible or prudent with a question, project or conversation. We have Annie to thank for that more than apt phrase "Leroy Standard Time."

Professionally he has shaped my sense of the responsibilities of being a teacher. I know of no greater champion of the power and importance of education as a transformative and democratic project. As many noted yesterday, he has touched the lives of thousands of students and done all kinds of institutional work quietly and without fanfare. He has rarely complained about overwork (even when he should have) or put his own 'career' before the needs of his students; he is a reminder that the public and private good cannot be divorced, and that ideas come to life between people. For Leroy kindness and critical rigor are not opposed virtues, but necessary bedfellows. In his orbit inquiry is not the work of a virtuosic soloist but of an ensemble of thinkers stretching across generations, continents, and disciplines.

Nearly everyone yesterday commented on his optimism and his uncanny ability to see possibility in the direst of situations (this is, as he has told me for as long as I can remember, all about keeping your eye on "the barely perceptible difference"). At times, I have found his faith to be baffling and sometimes hard to swallow. The recent wave of teachers' strikes and the rejection (belated as it may be) of the dangerous ideas they signal brought me back to something he has said to me often: democracy means radical faith in the capacities and intelligence of other people. His own faith in people is rooted in over 40 years of watching students rise to the occasion again and again. As he often says when justifying his syllabi and their considerable demands on undergraduates: if they don't know it's impossible, they just do it.

Retirement for Leroy *is an impossibility* because his work has always exceeded available notions of an academic career or job. For him, the project has been incredibly extensive, and it has always led well beyond the seminar room or the journal article. Many of us have heard him quip that you don't just find colleagues but that you invent them. Reflecting this morning as I listened to all of the wonderful remarks, I realized that this idea is more radical and generous than I previously thought because it implies both his recognition of the longstanding insufficiency of the institutional arrangements that are rapidly crumbling around us and of our capacity to rigorously imagine our way through it by recognizing each other as exactly the people required for the enormous work that is always ahead of us.

I am so proud of you Leroy and thankful you have chosen to make so many colleagues. Sending you all of my love. Onward!